Early & Late

Early & Late

FUGITIVE POEMS AND OTHERS

by Jesse Wills

VANDERBILT UNIVERSITY PRESS

Nashville

PRINTED IN THE UNITED STATES OF AMERICA

To Ellen

Preface

WHEN I was in college, and before, I occasionally wrote verse. The fall after I graduated from Vanderbilt, in 1922, this led to my being invited to join a group which had been meeting regularly in Nashville to read their poetry, and which published a little poetry magazine called *The Fugitive* from 1922 until 1925. This group has since acquired a minor sort of fame, and some of its members have become distinguished men of letters, but I will not try to retell the history of the Fugitives here. That can be found elsewhere. Being a member encouraged me to write more verses, and I produced a considerable number during my years of active association.

After the group broke up, whatever inspiration I had gradually died, and for many years I produced no verse except for a very occasional piece that might put a sentiment into rime for some special event. During these years I did keep up some contact with my old friends and continued to read poetry. I also have been a member of the Old Oak Club for many years, and more recently a member of the Coffee House Club. These Nashville literary clubs helped to keep me interested in some sort of writing.

In 1953, for no special reason, I again started to write serious verse, and since then I have produced nearly as much as was written during the years of my active Fugitive affiliation. It should be noted that this return to poetry began well before the Fugitive reunion, held in May, 1956, at Vanderbilt, though I am sure this meeting encouraged me to continue.

Contemplating these later poems and reviewing the older ones, I have sometimes wondered why either group was produced. All I can say is that they were written not so much to please myself, because so often I was not really pleased, but out of some sort of inner compulsion which did not extend to sharing them with anybody.

I did not want them, however, to be found merely as scattered typewritten sheets in my desk, and I did not like the alternative of destruction. Therefore, I decided to give them some more orderly and permanent form for a time, for the benefit of my family, my children's children, some of my friends and old associates, and others who might be interested. For the resulting book I make no claims except that it represents some part of me and of my life.

If there seems to be some lack of unity, or discontinuity between the first part and the second, this is because the book really combines what might have been two little volumes into one. Over the distance of so many years I found it hard to judge the early poems, and therefore hesitated a good deal over what to include and what to omit. Sometimes a poem has been included, not so much because of any merit I think it has, but because it illustrates a mood or state of mind I still remember as a point of emphasis in the history of my mental life. The majority, however, of the poems written during *The Fugitive* period have been included, with a very few written earlier or shortly after. A number of these were published in *The Fugitive*; and also eight poems ("The Survivors", "Automobile Ride", "A Fundamentalist", "Trinity", "Primavera", "Night Windows", "Riddle", and "To a Tired Clerk") were published in *Fugitives, an Anthology of Verse*, published by Harcourt, Brace & Company, New York, in 1928.

In order to maintain some sort of balance, I have included practically all the recent poems I have written so that the late portion is a collection whereas the other represents a selection. These last poems at times reflect my various interests; flower growing, birds, archaeology, the American Indian, the military and naval history of the Second World War, and they also show a considerable concern with matters of religion. I will not attempt, however, to repeat in prose what I tried to say in "Proem", which was deliberately written to precede both sections.

Contents

LATE POEMS (1953—1958)

Proem

PROEM

In my far youth I stumbled into verse
   Half accidentally, finding it no worse
(Or better because shorter) to compose
So as halfway to please me, than was prose.
I liked much poetry; verses that I read
Rehearsed their various music in my head;
It was a game to make words ring or chime
To fit the crossword puzzle of a rime.
In senior English I could depend upon it
To get good grades from Ransom with a sonnet.
And thanks to him and thanks to Allen Tate,
With whom I walked and read and led debate
Four college years, I was a Fugitive.

One of the group, yet one who could not give
Complete allegiance to something only felt
Not formulated, I sat and listened, spelt
In turn my part with poems passed out, read,
Enjoyed strong talk where wisdom sometimes fled
From nonsense, but I never wholly joined
The causes that they talked for.

                              Verses coined
By me seem clipped, or never quite complete;
I knew the silver of my gift was thin;
My muse too often walked on stumbling feet.
For praise or blame I cared not but within
I found release, catharsis, as I wrote;
My song was like a clearing of my throat.
So I am deeply grateful to those men,

3

My friends, who helped to keep me writing when,
Caught in a work I didn't exactly choose,
Caught in a course I wouldn't quite refuse,
Through times of trouble, arid and alone,
I found escape in word play. Out of stone
I made a bread that partly nourished me.
Out of enigma, out of futility,
I cherished dreams that built hope on the dire,
In peering far beyond catastrophe,
Cracking the world (Chicago gone like Tyre),
To ruined cities future nomads roam,
Or Indians and wilderness again.

A moon clear night, the benison of rain,
Eternity beyond times' metronome—
Reality, or books, gave me my themes—
Spring beauty, comi-tragedy that seems
To mock the meaning which one feels must press
Against the veils of death and emptiness.
So verse took form on paper, part derived
From echoes faint in memory, part contrived,
But sometimes pounded from me by a force
That would not let me sleep, and from this source
Beyond control, like flight, or cries of birds,
A life at times breathed movement in my words.

The thin flame or the need to feed it died;
I walked a calmer way more satisified
With life and work; I found companionship
With newer friends. Verses became a quip
To mark a party, grace a valentine.
And so began the years so long in line

From then to now, and yet those years are green,
Happy and crowded in perspective seen,
Living and fruitful. Love and marriage came;
Will-o-the-wisp became a household flame,
Lighting the hours that ever proved more fit
A dear alliance of the opposite.
Creation stayed in major, minor ways.
I found it pleasant to reshape older days
In furnishings and woodwork, Federal
To suit the taste of Jefferson in hall
Or portico, yet this stage was a home.
The children came, the children grew. From loam
I sought to raise new beauty into birth,
Essence of rainbows facing sun and shower,
Lifting crisp banners to be the fragile dower
Of iris generations. From the earth
I slowly learned the patience of the seed
Through frost and drouth, the rankness of the weed
That ever seeks to choke out what is fine.
Here, too, achievement fell below design.

Business is creation of a sort.
Decision turns on thinking; to distort
Attention from it is a business sin.
Clerks have been poets; their chiefs have seldom been.

For me verse writing went with solitude,
Like a cold spring in the woods, an interlude
Of unknown bird notes like a sounding bell.
I could not find this where the children played.
How could I find this? As a wave is stayed
By undertow, so office problems met

Head on with family cares. I was beset,
But happy in those days remembered well.

Children are gone, old Christmases a dream
Whose tree lights are reflections on a stream
Passing to darkness where carefully chosen toys
Float far away. Time hushed the childish noise.
It seems most strange that those green years are gone,
Leaving a mystery to meditate upon
That I should be the father of tall sons
And a fair daughter, each a self that runs
A unique course.

                              When quiet sifted back
Into the house, my mind turned to a track
It wandered long before. Thinking I might,
I tried, and found I'd still the knack to write
In rime and metre. Hence these verses late
To join the early, never in a spate,
But a thin trickle. The words come slowly, cloy.

I am in continuity with that boy
Who wrote before. Do I take up a pen
That he laid down and merely start again
To finish what he planned so long ago?
The form is like. The spirit? I don't know.
I look within more, draw a calmer breath
And am more tranquil contemplating death.

I would persuade myself that I rehearse
Poetic forms in hopes of better verse
Than these first exercises. False or true,
The odds say false, I know what I would do

Had I the gift. Past this small gain
There still looms far the goal I would attain.

Upon those times when the familiar scene
Takes on new light one starts to note between
The winking of an eye, that new strange light
I would catch frozen in a polished, white
Crystal of words where meaning, pattern, sound
Combine in depths of showing "This is Truth";
Geometry self proving it is sooth.
As snow takes various shape high over ground
I would shape a moment's vision from thin air,
Now irony, now wonder, now despair.
Around moth wings of beauty as I saw them,
Remembered as a vision from the dark,
Fluttering, frail, the patterns hard to mark,
I'd throw a net of words to help me draw them.

Thought may be subtle; if it be, the word
Should still be natural to it, not absurd,
Farfetched or strained in puzzle imagery.
My verse would open vistas, should not be
A hedge to break through, should be freshly wrought,
Yet not too alien from a reader's thought
Or on a different wave length from his mind.
Words are a code where one must send in kind.
Words are not coins worn smooth by too long use.
Words are like live things, weakened by abuse,
When worked too long within the same dull round,
But deathless or slow dying. When unbound
And fed with vision they are new once more,
Dear, and yet fresh as though not heard before.

Words are like creatures, not separate and lone,
Part of a species, each bears the undertone
And echo of inheritance and kin,
Pearl cores of meaning lying deep within.
A flower I pick today in form and hue
Is type of a flower my far ancestors knew
Yet different from each other of its seed
In minute ways. Likewise the old words breed
Fresh incarnations, taking life again
To shape a myriad patterns pleasing men.

As I would do, I have not, and I know,
No matter how I strive, I shall not look
From those high mountains, yet I choose to show
Some wanderings in the foothills, hence this book.

Early Poems

1922–1926

TO A TIRED CLERK

Do not despair, though you are clipped with chains
    Of petty drudging, clangor and grime will heal.
In loneliness your city's bones of steel
Will rust, green-tendoned; only the cool rains
Will whisper down old thunder-roads of trains;
And centuries long as today Nineveh counts
Will fret the marbles of old soda-founts
With sands which now are hotel window-panes.

It yet may be, when glittering frost has thinned
The leaves that hide, by westering yellow fires
Nomads, bronze-armed, shall note where mystery carves
Your firm's worn name, and dread their wizard sires,
Curbing their foam-necked horses, while their scarves
And ruddy hair are strung upon the wind.

THE HILLS REMEMBER

I LOOKED past hills as tumbled and as free
  As ocean waves and wondered that this wide
Inland, whose leagues no gulls have ever cried,
Should spell with glint of waters wood and lea.
For maples flashed their white wings mistily,
Like combers pluming from the forest tide;
A wheat bay crisped to ripples at each side;
And winds, dust-choked, bore dirges for the sea.

But at a beech tree's roots, coiled in the loam,
I saw limed whorls and tiny, twisted shells
Whose stony dreams unfroze to living bells,
With coral wreathed to gaud an oozy plain;
Then dreams unrolled the sun-green, ancient main,
One lazy dragon burnished by its foam.

CONSIDER THE HEAVENS

IF minds dream on when they have ceased to dwell
In the skulls Death has dried, perhaps each soul
First builds as faith permits that heavenly goal
It finds most comforting; thus asphodel
Blossoms the dreams of heroes; wood and fell
Red hunters roam; through Asgard rings the "Skoal";
Saints from their whispering harps faint thunders roll:
The morbid bathe in scarlet lakes of Hell.

All these are gone. Shall we, who try to play
Where they once prayed, be merely wound again
To golf and motor on some trivial plane?
Or shall we ride our nightmares through a gray
Eternity alone, too faithless even
In irony to build so fit a Heaven?

LIGHTNING'S BLINK

Anytime, between ledger and adding machine,
The moment may flash when the walls melt away
In the blaze of an instant, white, staggering, keen.
Then "self-conscious" is more than a word,
A live, burning thing. I float like a bird
Lost in measureless gulfs but supported by wings
Plumed of terror and joy. Through only a day,
So conscious of life, I could learn why I fell,
With the other souls cast from the sower Fate's hands
Through the times of all countries, not in ultimate lands
That tomorrow is hiding, not in Babylon dead
But in Nashville these decades. All riddles would clear
If that lightning could hold. In a wink it is sped,
And my brain quiets down to the buzz of its dreamings,
As once more I toil, a mechanical man,
Under drugs of the colors and dazed by the sounds
My day weaves around me, again in the bounds
Of the groove that I follow. Perhaps it is well.
The dull glow of noon is safer to bear
Than strange dawn or sunset on borders of night.
One wing was elation, the other was fear
That bore me through splendor towards where I could scan
Black nebular nothing. As dark flames the glare
Of the thunder's explosion when cloud armies fight,
So point to the stab of the single full breath
I can draw in my half life is horror of death.

ARLINGTON NATIONAL CEMETERY

Officers' Graves

PERHAPS a war blood-smeared them when they died
By tumbled foes; perhaps death made them yield
In peace; recalling what long years had steeled
A strength all vain, perhaps some cursed . . . or cried
Who cares? Old blades lie rusting side by side,
Where solemn beauty forgets death concealed
In a hush of endless green; they lift for shield
The cross of Him whom soldiers crucified.

Yet some, like knights who daintied war with rules,
Scorning the bloodless strife that fats the mart,
Lived lives of lonely honor mocked by fools,
Served pagan virtues with a Christian heart.
And texts are strange. Did He not say: "A sword
I bring, not peace." These took Him at His word.

DUST

STRANGE torments I have read of, boot and rack,
And fiercer tools to rip nerves from their beds,
Stretching pain out to endless fiery wire,
But not a terror of the darkest years
When souls were saved by burning flesh away,
No pang of inquisition, no Huron torture pole,
Equalled the terror of the dream I dreamed.

A man condemned—it was yet was not I—
By one decrepit judge who drooled upon
His fumbled papers mustier than the skin
Gummed tight across his bones, a man condemned
Half stood, half crouched within a narrow cell,
Forgotten, or the proof of some mistake,
A jest that turned out bad, not to be told,
Forgotten save by Time who claimed his due.

Out of the crannies of the patchwork walls,
Out of the cracks above him always fell
A tireless dust that powdered on his hair
And stuffed his clothes to blotters on his flesh.
Worse than the torture of the measured drops
—Water at least was clean, water was cool—
Was this slow torture of the dribbling grains.
The probing rays of light were granular,
Empty and crowded, models of the dance
That atoms hold through wood, through blood, through stones,
    through stones,
Beyond, beneath all meaning. Desert air
Swirled through the parching nostrils to his lungs,
Depositories of loess that shortened breath.

And food they brought him, good before it came,
Beneath that fall of dust's unseasoning,
Grew ashes in his mouth; his drink turned mud.

Almost before his eyes the masonry
Crumbled apart and yet in crumbling kept
Reserves of strength enough to hold him fast,
As though its particles were tributary
To a main stream of waste that trickled from
Dark attics that were bins where mummied years
Lay piled to rot above.

               Day out, day in,
Seen and unseen like midges in their swarm,
One grain unheard in falling, myriad grains
Susurrant in his ears, one mote unfelt,
Together like a groping, scaly hand
That merely fingered, never clenching tight,
Incessant, always, always the dust fell;
Sometimes so slowly that his prison seemed
Time's giant hour-glass built for measuring
The change of Saturn hours, again so fast
When, rarely, wind rose up to clasp the tower,
Hissing through fissures, making the vaults groan,
His fear was nearly hope that the quick sand
Would mould above his head a certain end.
But always, ignominious, the wind failed,
Sucking the dust away through cracks below
Till in his normal cloud he stood reprieved. . . .

It was a picture, durationed in a dream,
Cut off, like a film breaking, before the close,
And whether the dull hope that tarnished there

Brightened again in freedom, or whether death
That threatened so above him thundered down
As all collapsed, or whether nothing fell
But the slow dust, sifting or gusting still
When life was dried away, I do not know.

PREMONITION

THE friendly milestones passing waved me on;
The road ahead was level as behind,
The plain as green; what need had I to mind
Grim tales sent back by those who once had gone
This way? Could that bright, careless gold
Of dandelions, those grackles glittering,
Sun-purpled, or the meadow larks awing,
Portend a scoriac desert, chasms, and cold?

Nonsense! Yet for the moment trees had grown
A little denser so that the dark fires died
From grass and leaves. Earth shook as if it snored,
Troubled with dreams of thunder, and I spied
Far aff above a pale wall, cloud or stone,
Brandished, the yellow lightning of a sword.

FEAR

I

Just as a child, alone in some old house,
  Sees, mimicking fire's petty rise and fall,
Gray shadows in a dance upon the wall,
With the hoot and groan of wind tonguing their rouse,
And, watching them uncomforted, endows
The forms with might till nothing's real save tall,
Cold shadows with his own the prince of all,
Goblins that play at pounce, cats with a mouse.

So he, jailed in the dimness of his brain
Saw crouched along its walls a leering host;
The spectra of old worry, doubt, and pain;
And by fear's glare that only lit the gloom
Each new sensation shadowed up a ghost
To join that death watch boding secret doom.

FEAR

II

Now he was one must always seek the cause.
He sought it here in memories of sin,
And cursed himself, who else to curse, that in
His mind such horror capered. Nature's laws
Or God's he'd broken, and as remembrance draws
What one demands Mea Culpas grew a din
For sins puffed Nero-monstrous. Thus the thin
Grey cortex opened out—infernal maws.

And there as Rhadamanthus on his throne
With iron brow he told doom like a bell;
And as the guilty soul he felt each bone
Ache, fire eternal; lastly as the fell
Executor, as a baboon whirls a stone,
Himself hurled self to the utmost pit of Hell.

DREAM

Reeling and lost, "What feast is this?" I cried.
Round the courts their laughter, thinner than the breeze
Through the poplar lanes whose dark geometries
Had brought me, hushed, and their soft voices died.

Over the basalt walls a phosphor glow
Shone in and out in figures, angle, square.
A faint sound tiptoed with the shadow where
A fountain tossed its wine in pools of snow.

The silken forms were frozen, raised aloft
Or leaning to bright lips the cups remained,
While through the dusk their calm, pale faces flamed
Like candles in no wind. Their eyes were soft,

Yet steadier than planets deep in space;
I felt they knew me now but also whence
I came and why and weighed the consequence,
Reading my fate in that of all my race.

"Your birthday, Prince?" I faltered to their host,
A youth upon a fox-fire paneled dais;
His robes commingled Autumn scarlets, grays,
And in his hair gleamed gems as cold as frost.

Then like a statue pealing, from his throne
He answered: "From your world where knowledge gleams
So thinly through the mist, a maze of dreams
Has led you to our land where all is known.

"That birth of mine we feast is not of breath
But one scrolled surely on those calendars;"
And from his robe a pale arm showed the stars,
"This night, this hour, I am one year under death."

PARABLE

PHAON the sculptor made it long ago,
Lived years in carving out a single hand
From mellowed ivory; all of a god's command
He wrought in one bright gesture, sure and slow.
And as he finished foreign swords whirled down
To slash his town to ruins; Phaon died;
But with his bones, and ashes of the pride
Red fires had humbled, the hand slept underground.

When Hartmann, archaeologist, lay bare
The tapering fingers lipped by earth and time
He merely grieved in searching everywhere
For the sure body. This artists have restored
Some thirty ways, though groans are still outpoured
Upon our loss, and cursed is the vandal's crime.

DISCOVERY

Ditchers near Paris chanced upon a grot
Where hidden, thirty-fold, lay shapes of death;
Men, women, children, who'd drawn stifled breath
And died, so long ago that not a jot
Care the police what unrecorded plot
In wars religious pent them in the dark.
Some ponder, but the centuries left no mark
To tell why Catholic or Huguenot

Prayers ended so. I clipped and put away
Some three years back this item from the *Times,*
Charmed by the bones and thinking I would pay
Some tribute to their misty woe in rimes,
Then quite forgot it till I happened on
This yellowed paper, seeking a collar button.

AGRIOCHAERUS

(A climbing ungulate of the Oligocene)

AGRIOCHAERUS, neither pig nor sheep
Were you; fantastic prophet of them both,
Through feral brakes of Tertiary sloth,
Some sportive chance taught you to feed and sleep
Scathless in tree tops where you dodged the leap
Of ivory-sabred cats by dint of claws,
And flexing shanks, as apes by other laws
Survived through flexing wits upon your steep.

Let those who must have bulk to be impressed
Raise from the sere rocks of their dreadful rest
The thunder lizard's bones; from all life's tide,
I take you, sheepish pig with power to climb,
As question mark to dusty chance and time;
The wits enduring hail the wrist that died.

AUNT MINNIE

I: D. A. R.

WHEN leaves dust veiled are drooping to the street,
Her drawn shades guard Aunt Minnie in her room;
There, fan awing before her in the gloom,
Day long she chirps her tirades at the heat.
When snow, not dust, is white about our feet,
Her theme's reversed; the cold will be her death;
She lets no frost blow silver on her breath;
Steam-toasted, snug, she chatters with the sleet.

And still she glories in her liberty,
Knowing her patriot forbears made her free,
A house-bound prisoner to a single cloud;
And while her wrath at kaisers shakes her form,
Forgetting man's first freedom, she lives cowed,
Slave to the primal lords, the sun and storm.

AUNT MINNIE

II: NATURE LOVER

Y ou really should have seen the squirrel stand,
Eating the muffin. It was too absurd."
I smile a little, just to show I heard,
And murmur something. In Aunt Minnie's hand
She waves her glass with which she sways her land,
Proprietress of every migrant bird,
And Homer could not catalogue a third
Of all her flowers. "Isn't nature grand!"

Like fishing boats the tall clouds scudding blow,
Sweeping their nets of shadow where below
The air drifts cool, and trees are tremulous
To greet the crystal vanguard of the rain.
But thunder merely echoes Auntie's fuss,
The crash of every closing window-pane.

AUNT MINNIE

ROMANCE—some find it in the obscure ways
 The lives of men can rarely break the rust
Of years and gem a memory in the dust,
Before and after, of one brief hero blaze.
And some, who seek it, chant the wistful praise
Of times when knights went clinking forth to just
For ladies amorous of a deft spear thrust.
Aunt Minnie loved those quaint-appareled days.

But now a mystery gallops in the news
Of midnight compacts sworn against our foes,
With solemn oaths that kings and lawyers use,
By hooded hosts, while fiery crosses dance.
Aunt Minnie reads, and in her eyes life glows,
Fanned by the shivering thrill of high romance.

AUTOMOBILE RIDE

STEP on the gas! On through the night
Our motor drones in ceaseless flight
Though from what we cannot tell,
Maybe Heaven, maybe Hell.
But long it's kept a neutral way
Thus pleasantly while rabbits play
In our head-lights. We hum down hills
Choristered with whippoorwills,
Speed through meadows, moonlight streaks,
Over hidden rustling creeks,
On through dreamy perfumed grain,
And on and on until we gain
The crossroads by three waterfalls.
"Right, Right!" a night bird calls.

But to the left the road is straight,
So we go scooting, sure as fate,
Into the valley, leave the right,
Climbing curves a lonely height.
Our whoops ring loud; we're on the go
Somewhere we guess. Who wants to know?
And still we force the gas to feed
Our motor on to speed, more speed,
To keep the dusty blood a-racing.
Mile and minute now are pacing
Even down through solitude,
Through clotted darkness cedars brood,
Till from the hollow of the owls,
Warning us a devil prowls,
We swerve into a luminous,

Perfect, arched bituminous
Highway where marching standards loom,
Each clasping like a leper moon
A ball of snow where glow-worms coil
To light these rigid miles of oil
That wake our chorus: "This is better,
Step on her, kid." We step and let her
Flicker on from sixty higher.
A wind is cracking whips of fire.
A roaring darkness tells its beads;
Pearl after pearl of light recedes,
So endlessly the lamps extend,
Though we'd held eighty hour on end
It seems to us, grown tired a bit;
And laugher dies until a fit
Of silly laughter seizes one
Who giggling shouts: "Ain't we got fun?"
And shouting points: "Look over yonder,
See the happy fields we wander,
Tin can, bottle, mattress, pot,
A soulless waste where bodies rot,
And gaze ahead. Tall chimneys spout
A crimson breathing. 'Neath the knout
Of smoke and over clinker loam
Our steed is straining to her home."
Now suddenly his face is rime:
"Whistles, whistles, not a chime!
If it was from Hell we came
We're circling backward to the flame."

SNOW PRAYERS

I

OFTEN the old men tell me winters bring
No storms like those of days when they were young,
When over ice their eager strength was flung
Through coils of wind, daring the sleet to sting.
"In sixty-nine, in eighty. . . !" Dead years ring
With blizzards, rivers frozen; wagging tongue,
Beard like a city drift, and wheezy lung
Mourn times corrupt, and change a bitter thing.

Even I, who know how memory can glean
And gild a spoil from waste years few as mine,
Watching beneath the rain the grasses green,
Like old men flushed by dreams another tells,
Hold, frost on fur, from darkness this design:
Fields hurtling white, a sleigh with crystal bells.

SNOW PRAYERS

II

PERHAPS the glacier North does melt again
Before a South that crawls up mile by mile,
Season by season, ebbing and flood; a while,
And orchid and palm will choke each cedar glen,
Wierd toucan mock the silence of the wren
Where Cumberland enfolds the crocodile,
Till all the North embower a south sea isle
To wreathe the languid years of the elder men.

Hunting for flints, I've learned where coral seas
Hid shells before, where ice-packs gnawed a boulder,
And thanked the Norns who cast me nearest these.
Blow, wind that swirls round me, colder, colder.
Ghosts on the light, bright dancers on the brown,
Slash the gray clouds to white flakes curling down.

SNOW PRAYERS

III

For was it sunlight or the stinging cold
Gave men strength of the bow far-smiting, fire,
That heart of pride, baked meats to their desire,
Drove lazy apes to a cavern's lordly hold.
There, while the glaciers gnashed pale fangs, they rolled
Sweet thunders from the drums; there danced the troth
Of love or war; there painted stag and mammoth;
Heard the first gods howl among pines ermine-stoled.

War dead, and stilled the clangor of his crimes,
I think in lands unborn the poet's tunes
Will ring through misted centuries the times
When the lotus folk shall stir to a ghostly woe,
Glimpsing across dim gardens and lagoons,
White-winged, their boreal heritage of snow.

RED EVEN

Beyond the chimneys by dark council fires
Crouch plumed and painted forms cloud-blanketed;
Small owls moan incantations to the dead,
And feathered shadows leap forth to their choirs
Through parks and lawns; bats loop around the wires
In swastikas down avenues outspread
Where tar binds earth that pulses to the tread
Of moccasins among the spinning tires.

O Burghers, telephones and radio
Are noisy charms, yet night is stronger far,
And picture shows and bridge will not avail
Against the green flints of some archer star
Always to keep your dreams from knowing woe,
Darkness and fear that made your fathers pale.

"Bat, Bat, fly in my cap," a boy cries,
Tossing his cap in the air. Sunset is gone.
Now evening smoothes the street into gray glass
Where should be asphalt. The bats wheel and spin,
As over water, over its level stream,
Bats that the wizard shadows have called out
To hawk again a never-failing game,
In ghost-like scorn of wires looping their ways.

"Bat, Bat, fly in my cap!" Run, little boy;
Call other children out to play such games
As Hide and Seek or Pig in the Gutter; chant
The last of the abracadabras serving
A purpose, "Eeny Meeny Miny Moe,"
Or perhaps "Onery Ory Ickery Ann."
These are white magic; you attempt the black.
I am not sure, but fear stirs in my hair,
If you should catch one tameless hunter so,
In this gray dusk when stars are few and chill,
You might catch all the wilderness again.
This tar-compacted road would melt away
In oily rainbows fading into mist
Under dim arches of the beech and oak,
The strictured miles once more released and huge,
Your dog that heels you changed back to a wolf,
And every slinking cat turned cat-a-mountain.

Without a pause in their elliptic dance
The bats would hawk their never-failing game,
But what would we do who dwell snugly where
The mazdas conquer dark? How could we eat

If no milk wagons clattered through the dawn,
No grocers brought the treasures of their tins
Prompt to each meal? How could we kill the hours
Now slain divinely by those radios,
Each plucking favored tunes from many chords
Lacing the wind, if we heard only wind
Susurrant in an endlessness of leaves,
Or, in rare moons, drums of the Cherokee?
How could we live if all our deft machines
Were still a nightmare in the brain of Time,
Asleep above green Eden? Stop, little boy!
"Bat, Bat, fly in my cap!" He just missed then.
Thank God, here comes a car. He'll have to go.

PRIMAVERA

Our lady of the clatter keys,
   Your fingers flash on steel today
As though they woke from ivories
A softer cadence than you play.

The minutes chip upon the hours,
But you type on unweariedly,
Or pour fresh water on your flowers,
Humming a tune time dances by.

In terse dictations of the trade
Black letters fall like soot on snow;
Your eyes are brown pools in a glade
Where glinting visions weave and go.

Of rumored spring we see that line
Deep blue above the cliffs of stone;
The sparrows chirp in the sunshine,
The sparrows chirp and pigeons moan.

And you rejoice, That cloudy blue
Is webbed and clouded in your dress;
Our granite spring is green to you
And you translate its loveliness.

You laugh beneath the mazda suns;
Your voice is like a windy bell;
In a white dance each finger runs
A naiad on the stairs of hell.

NIGHT WINDOWS

Now all the living gold of sunlight poured
World under, gilding temples in Rangoon,
Drips round me in a lucent silver hoard
Refracted from chill mirrors of the moon.
Now in the dusk of tree caves it is stored
While shadow, like a moth from its cocoon,
Creeps out around the pale vault starry-floored,
Where bats are tumbling to a windy tune.

Now, magic-webbed, the homes of men are changing
To crags and scarps a lunar frost adorns;
That far enameled road's a glacier way
Where dragon motors hiss by, softly ranging,
Or on some quest off darting through the gray
Night that spins out to silver yapping horns.

A FUNDAMENTALIST

H^{E'D} as soon believe in protozoa as fairies,
He'd seen them both. The one a lens had showed
In a water drop like specks before the eye,
And as for the other, well, that dusk of May,
It might have been a bird's wings he had seen
Flickering so in the twilight, but he thought
Small forms had danced, where lilacs wove a bower,
Thanksgivings for the dark that made him doubt,
In livery streaked gray-green and lavender.

He found the tomes of science just as charming,
Or nearly so, as any tales he'd read
From fairy history, correlated even.
These on the creatures of a spawning time
Were textbooks in the anatomy of dragons
Whose blood had dyed the sunsets of his dreams.
Geology was wizard's lore of lifting
Jotuns and dwarfs out of the elder dust,
Issue of wars by God and Satan joined
For continents now only to be seen
By planets on the drifting edge of light
Where the wan glow our universe once spun
Melts in the glory of the farthest nebula,
Volute of worlds and suns.

                            For he believed
In the white magic of astronomy,
Yet also held those gulfs that cool the stars
And spaces blurred behind the Milky Way
Were a windy palace for the hosts of God,
Whose wings were surely swifter than his thought,

Leaping from dinosaurs to Cherubim,
Or from the circling fires of Perseus
To the drops of rain that glinted on a leaf,
Each host, maybe, to worlds of protozoa.
Let telescopes pry out upon the moon
Dead seas and plains, volcanic, awful cones
Mapped on a crusty bubble of pale glass,
He'd look and marvel, but as surely knew,
When in Jehovah's brain the will should burn
For the long reels of pictured time to close,
And for the dust of Earth to multiply
In life again the countless roles it played,
That through the stars Lord Gabriel would shoulder
To carve the hollow moon into a horn
And call up ghosts of every storm that blew
To wind him for Earth's final trumpet blast.

TRINITY

To the Controversialists

AROUND the tower-looming tree
Paced an ape, a man, and God.
Strange as dream or memory
In an orbit there they trod

Through a gloom where leaves aflutter
Kept somewhere numberless a throng
Whence voices drifted, broken mutter,
Quarrel, cry, and wailing song.

Red-eyed in a nostriled face
And knuckling on a bludgeon arm,
The ape came, bowing to his place
Man whose glances of alarm

Leaped to joy in journeyings
From stars night errant to the sod;
Heralded by chiming wings
Gleamed the ivory limbs of God.

While rattling still the voices came:
"O Blasphemy! The beast's a lie."
And mockery tangled with acclaim
To trip the man who faltered by.

And for the boding, chiseled grace,
The eyes that burned the halo breath
To fix the lightning years of space,
One whisper: "Hide, the face of Death."

So God bemused in dreams of birth,
Man with his back to deity,
And ape, all shaggy as the earth,
Wove with its wrinkles round the tree.

Were these the first, were those the last,
Hairy, human, holy, feet?
I pondered while went dancing past
Father, son, and paraclete.

THE SURVIVORS

HE first spoke. "North, we will go north," he cried.
Thence came the rolling loveliness of wind
That, trickling from a maple's silver side,
Was purling down to lave them. She half pinned
Into a crown the torrents of her hair
That tangled with the sunlight on the bark
Of those old trees. So this had been the dark
And weary end of wandering despair,
This sunny orchard corner. When she woke
There he had been asleep on the lush grass,
And she had spread the tatters of her cloak
To shield him from the mist until the glass-
Clear, gradual morn was painted snow and blue.
But he had roused at length, and now the two
Were pondering what morning had revealed,
A new earth and each other. Across a field
A rabbit bounced a white tail. Overhead
In a leafy gloom, green-gold or flushed with red,
Great apples burned, and warblers rose and fell
Like tiny flames where the shafts of sun were warm.

They had forgotten much and it was well.
Horror was dim as some dream of a storm
That had killed itself in sleet dead months before.
Breasting the wind, she let its huge wave pour
Through the lacework of her rags to wash each limb
Clean of the webby past.

              "What is your name?
I have forgotten mine," she laughed to him.

He frowned and shook his head, his mind the same,
A veil that dread could stir but could not break,
A darkness that no will of his could goad
Into a form. From ashes in the road,
With other trash that flight left in its wake,
(Lacquered in green a smashed car fell to rust,
Now vine-geared to the rhythms of the dust
And hung with scarlet horns) a stray gust whirled
A page from some burnt volume, singed and curled.
She gloried that he was strong, cat-muscled, proud,
Noting his arm out flashing to retrieve
The fragment as it fluttered. With head bowed
He studied it, then turned, and smiling took
The apple that she proffered. "Lady, look!
Here are names will do, mine Adam and your's Eve."

HEALING

Out of a cloudy purple rain drops fret
    The slate-blue asphalt to a dancing sea,
Streaking the motor's lacquer, scatter free,
First silver seed, then arrows to beset
That iris phalanx flaunting colors yet,
Fill puddles full for sparrow jubilee,
And almost cleanse the brain and nerves of me
From rasping cares the hotter hours beget.

Rain falls on just and unjust? Yes, and rain
Has fallen so on every age and land
To leave this chill delight in thinking on
What prototypes of each now-crystal chain
Have rustled over fires of Genghis Khan,
Rusted the brazen greaves of Zenophon.

RIDDLE

Easy! Too easy your answers, ye who cling
Each to one feather of the pinioned All
That beats us on through Time, too several
The Truths ye grasp by simple reckoning,
Now rousing hope till alleluias ring
That one plume's fair, now plotting from a small
Dissected quill the whole mechanical,
The shape unseen, heart urging on the wing.

My figure for It's bird because It flies,
Swept on by varied plumage of quick laws,
Each nothing or a toy reft from the flock,
Real only thus inwoven, and because
The question waits on laughter, with the wise
Like squabbling Sinbads dangling from the Roc.

TO THE BUGLE UNBLOWN

THERE is a dearth of bugles in the land,
Though full-lunged brasses and too many drums
Proclaim a noise for noise's sake, never comes
A single voice that rings a clear command.
Cry out. Cry out. We wait on every hand,
Like sullen coals that wait a wind to flame,
Sure only that the cause you will proclaim
Must lift us from the marshes and the sand.

How many are behind the cobweb bars
Of trivial labors and a thin routine
Who, stupid from the buzz of the machine,
Mistake for you a false, deluding cry,
And so through boredom march off to the wars
That will not cease while self deceived they die.

Late Poems

1953–1958

REVERY

THERE are far places no ship will ever take me,
And little, hidden valleys close at hand
I'll never wander, never never land
On this or that shore: yet, ere life forsake me,
I'll add new treasures to the ones that wake me
With pictures in the mind; blue waves expand,
The mountains gleam, the storied cities stand
In that kaleidoscope which memories shake me.

A parrot preens upon a tropic isle,
Burning one flame of color no one sees:
This and a myriad sights I shall not know.
What matter? Do I look enough the while,
Through snow and ebon arabesques of trees,
In my own yard, red, blue wings come and go?

INCOGNITO

HE had a troubling gift for finding words
Whose music carried meaning toward a dim,
Strange, shadowed world of magic. At his whim,
Their drumming feet rolled like the bison herds
On savage plains; again they soared like birds,
Chanting aloft; yet never suited him
Who would translate the songs of seraphim.
His verses shattered, failed, like broken sherds.

They would not do, but still he disliked waste
So old, worn plots took on new depth and sting
From such high verbiage, heard and yet ignored,
As though the actors wore, instead of paste,
True jewels. But why bother; the crowd roared;
No author need be when the play's the thing.

MIRACLE

How many myriad Springs lie dead beneath
The thin rind of the current Spring's veneer?
Somewhere, somehow, all that once lived is here.
These quickening herbs are but a funeral wreath
For light-year generations; bog and heath
Are crypt for mammoth, tiny things and great;
The cloven hills betray the bony freight
That hecatombs of dinosaurs bequeath.

Old, and so worn, so used, so second hand,
No trillionth hand, it should be but a screen
Hiding all death, and yet this Spring is new!
Fresh is the air, vivid the tender green,
The sunlight golden, and the sky as blue
As though a morn of Eden waked the land.

QUESTION MARK AND ELEGY

LOST, lost, and all forgotten, drowned in time
Lie scattered by the rushing of the years
How many ancient races, works and ways?

Who laid a chief's bones in a box of stone,
His wife and children later on nearby,
And heaped up earth above them, in due time
Adding new dead until the mound was full
Beside the pyramid where solemn rites
Renewed the sacred fires the temple hid?
How long was it before that fire went out?

No one can tell us how or when or why
The warriors left their ramparts, squaws their huts.
Opossums, foxes, squirrels had good shelter
Before the winter rains, the summer storms
Beat down the lodges with their wattled walls
'Till mound rings hid the ashes of old fires
Where had gone round the laughter and the games.

Leaves fell and mouldered, fell and mouldered, fell
From trees that grew and died and grew again.
One had four hundred rings the farmer noted
Who cut it down and dug within the mound
In eighteen forty-five. He stared, perplexed,
At death's queer dowry hidden with the bones:
Grotesquely shapen pots, thin sheets of mica,
Chipped ceremonial blades, gorgets of shell.
Some curious things he kept until the fire
Consumed them with his home a decade later.

The graveyard where he lies is far away.
You cannot read the stone.

From time to time
Others would glean about the mounds. One came
Upon an idol but mostly flints were turned
Up by the plow until the nineties brought
A careful digger, connoisseur of eld,
Less scientist than antiquarian,
Who dug and loved and listed treasure trove,
Confounding with the people of the mounds
More ancient graves which lay deep years below
And a wandering hunter's bones which lay above—
Intrusion from what later Indian tribe?
Where are the skeletons which these dug up
From Earth's dim closet, where the tools and gear?
Some have gone back to earth in crumbled dust
Or ashes scattered: a few are hid away
With boys' forgotten trophies, bird eggs, stamps.
Seven numbered skulls on one museum shelf
And nine upon another gather dust.
The points, the spades, the ear plugs, broken clay,
The curious, nameless things so carefully made,
Boat stones, and banner stones, cones, hemispheres,
(or so we call them guessing at their use)
Are neat within glass coffins row on row.
Others in basement boxes stored away
Await what resurrection from the dark?

These brown and broken things are like the bones.
They are bones too, of culture; what the face
And form were like they hint but cannot tell.

The cold flint keeps its edge undulled, unworn,
But also keeps its secrets, whose the hands
That chipped it, fastened spear point to the haft.
The flesh, the souls that once made real these things,
The people and the languages they spoke,
The chieftains, traders, high priests, fighting men,
The victors and the vanquished in their wars,
The rites, the dances, legends that they told,
The gods they prayed to and the prayers they said
Are scattered by the rushing of the years,
Lost, lost and all forgotten, drowned in time.

THE WATCHERS

Beneath the super market's neon glow,
The goods high piled, the hands, the scuffling feet;
Beneath the asphalt of the outside street,
The parking cars; stone coffined in a row,
Holding their tools, an arrow point, a hoe,
The dead sleep by their pots of figured clay.
The hills beyond, our link with yesterday,
That watch us now, once saw these long ago.

Dark in the twilight, green in varied Spring,
In Autumn's war paint—soil too thin to plow—
Hills that recall the tom-toms whispering,
You lifted up your feather crest of trees,
Changeless above mound builder mysteries.
What will you see five centuries from now?

I HAVE KNOWN MANY

THIS is a Christmas day in Tennessee:
A landscape soft in greens and browns and grays,
Clean washed by rain, the hills a bluish haze
Against a gray wool sky. There shrub and tree
Lift their bare twigs to weave a tracery
Pointed with cedars above the lighter green
Where pasture meets with plough land; in between
Gray walls and sheep. In this tranquillity

Is an old peace; the only sounds the twitter
Of small gray birds; brown towhees scratch the litter;
There is the ancient tinkling of sheep's bells;
The rain drops are a chain of crystal shells
Upon that tree where, like a spun glass ball,
There shines the color of a cardinal.

OLD LEAVES

D<small>EEP</small> in the hollow where the stump protects them,
   High piled and brown are leaves of long gone summers,
Tulip tree, oak and the pale stars of sweet gum,
Once green and living in the drowse of summer,
Knowing the vireo and the warblers flitting.
Gone is their Spring green and gone the fires of Autumn.
What chance kept off the rain and Winter's snow
That melted countless others into mould,
The soft deep earth that nourishes today
The leafy generations of the year?

Brown too and brittle are these forgotten letters,
Hid in a box with a once stylish gown.
Bright was the day when this was carefully written
And warm the love of wife to distant husband.
I cannot understand this casual reference,
That nickname, trivial matters lost in time.
That Mother and her kindred and dear children
(old ladies that I once knew long ago)
Have all been gone a far time back to earth.
What chance half saved these moments out of time
From many chequered days once real and living?

Burn the brown leaves, tear up the brittle pages;
The sap, the green are gone—what need to save them;
Burn too the letters that our love has written;
No time unborn can really feel our day.
We can compost the leaves of this year's summer;
Words are not leaves; better the fire to end them,
And the thin smoke to carry dreams away.

SALUTE TO T. L. T.

1862—1954

At eighty years of age he planted trees;
The walnut and the hickory lent their pride;
The pin oak and the maple joined the tide,
Green flowing round his home of memories.
At ninety years of age he added these:
White dogwood and paulownia purple vied
To deck the Spring with beauty; ere he died
He raised to years unborn these legacies.

His life was tree-like, rooted in the earth,
Head lifted skyward, hiding the old scars,
With rings of growth, accepting woe and mirth
Like sun and storm. He sleeps beneath the stars
While memory wakes anew an old phrase taught us:
"A tree standing by the river of waters."

TIME WORN

His was the slow death age distills for some,
  Sapping the strength, dissolving the mind's powers,
Until the pontiff soul no longer towers
Sure of its rule. Though doubts began to come,
Admitting naught to fight, he fought the numb
Demission of the will, the cloud that lowers
Across the brain, until relentless hours
Drained pride away, left only vacuum.

Better the lightning stroke than this dull end.
He once was man, this mimic of a child.
Recall his prime, let memories warm the heart.
Here is no dying fire—be not beguiled—
These are no coals which still can warmth impart,
But only ashes drifting in the wind.

PICTURES OUT OF FRAME

Down the green shoulder of the slope I saw them come,
Out of the mist a host in movement, some
On horseback, others walking, spears agleam
Where young men went in front, and then the stream
Of women, old folk, children, bleating flocks.
Some were so close a horse shied at the rocks
Where I seemed hid. I wondered, could not know
What tribe this was, thus migrant, long ago,
Or yet to be? The day was cold; a froth
Of cloud hung low. Cimmerian, Scythian, Goth,
Keltic or Tartar, with drums and horns immense,
Feathers, dyed robes, and strange accoutrements,
The horde poured on, and was no more, was gone
Within the fog. The vast green downs were lone.
Hard to be sure of shield mark, helmet crest,
Yet how sharp were some faces on me pressed,
Alien and fierce, but individual,
Barbaric, real, then gone beyond recall.
Somewhere in time it happened; caught some way,
As in a crystal's facet, this array,
Mirrored and turning in eternity,
Was for a breath coincident with me;
Another image from a broken glass,
As on the day I saw the chariot pass,
On the Roman road, and despite his pace,
And the whirling dust veils knew the driver's face.

DEVIL'S ADVOCATE

PERVERSITY within me makes me stay
Apart, whatever speakers I may hear;
Even though the cause is close to me and dear,
I still must challenge, question what they say.
Aside, within, I do this, silent weigh,
Together with the brave talk people cheer,
Elisions and the half truths that would clear
The complex into simple yea or nay.

But while I may be stinting with applause,
I neither join with those who boo or hiss.
What Atlas bears up verity's full load?
Some truth must pad out even the blackest cause,
And he who thinks he walks the straightest road
Goes stumbling on the edge of the abyss.

THE METAL FROM THE ORE

THE metals were once mixed with alien things;
Thus iron was a rust within the rocks
Men melted out to make swords, plowshares, locks,
And out of clay, aluminum took wings
To cleave the air; now a chill wisdom brings
Uranium's ever burning sparks together
Like flecks of hell collected from the nether;
Out of the trash of earth the bale fire stings.

All these are freed. What formulae unbind
Quicksilver spirit and the golden mind
From dross and slag? They find no skill to shatter
Whatever ties them to the facts of matter.
Only in dreams do they lift from the ground,
Only in dreams is freedom ever found.

THE HALF MEN

I'VE heard or read that only half our brain
Is used; I know that less than half our powers
May serve us even in our keenest hours;
In a half sleep we toil for our small gain.
A stupor numbs our pleasure, dulls our pain.
We do mechanically the things we should.
Besotted, slow in evil or in good,
We mainly serve the trivial and inane.

Down through the generations, dust to dust,
The dream endures that we, the inmost self,
Can break the bindings of our stifling crust,
Be wide awake, and, surer than an elf
Striding the rainbow over a waterfall,
See, hear, smell, taste, touch, know the full of all.

ARMAGEDDON

WE who are half blind still must try to see,
We who are crippled still must walk or crawl,
Toward what we are not sure. It may be all
Illusion or chimera. Let it be.
Even upon a treadmill we are free;
Worse are the chains designed to hold us still.
As the mole swims in dirt so some strong will
Keeps us in motion toward our destiny.

We must take sides though none is wholly white;
The darkest day is brighter than a cave.
As you draw sword and plunge into the fight,
Pray for the good beyond ignoble ends;
Do not confound the cruel with the brave;
Know that our foes were meant to be our friends.

THOMASON THE HISTORIAN

THOMASON, the Historian, knows by heart
The strategy, the tactics, each fierce charge
And stubborn defense that made Gettysburg
Great among battles, decisive in its war;
Yet new facts might be found, so thresh the chaff
To make another book to prove a theory.

Were there not grandsons of the men who fought there
With marines at Belleau Wood, at St. Mihiel,
Who broke wire and machine guns in the Argonne
Staining the clay with blood? It does not matter.

Thomason's a Civil War Buff of the best;
He joins their clubs; he corresponds afar
North and to South. He knows the specialist
On every battle and can join debate
On each long argued question, when and where.

Valiant the boys in gray, the men in blue.
Give them due honor for the heritage
That came down with the blood so freely spent,
From Saratoga, the Plains of Abraham,
Roundhead and Cavalier, the yelling clansmen,
Beating their claymores on the levelled pikes.
The blue and gray were brave; still proving this
In an unceasing tide, the books still come.

Were it not well for Thomason to thank
The God of Battles that their courage still endures
To the third generation? Why should not
These names blow bugles too, Tarawa,

Bataan, Guadalcanal, Midway, Saipan,
Iwo Jima, Okinawa, Normandy?

It was a little island, coral rimmed.
The tide was tricky; boats fell short the beach;
The sands were blood, the waters blood, the storm
Of fire incessant; the foe would not
Surrender and died hard; yet they kept on
Till all that stench was theirs. A little isle,
Tarawa, in the waste of tropic sea.

I think of jungles on a larger isle
Where tired men held a thin perimeter
Against all out attack, endured the bombs,
The nightly shelling and in the muggy dark
Watched, guessing who might win and who might lose,
Confusion and destruction, as the dim
Task forces met; nightly, time after time
Fire lanced the black, guns rumbled with the thunder
In a mad melee where the torpedoes crossed
Their tracks of foam, and shells high arched above
Exploded angry death. Call out the roll,
Call the proud names of ships that fought and died
Like duelists stabbing in a blacked-out room,
Or crept away at dawn to hide their wounds;
Too many names, but some keep searchlights on them;
Remember these, *Vincennes, Astoria, Quincy,*
That perished in that first wild night off Savo,
Ill-starred *Juneau,* and sister ship *Atlanta,*
Like *San Francisco,* an admiral's funeral pyre.
These ships that rust in Iron Bottom Sound
Trace back to a Hampton Roads encounter when

The Turtle met the Cheese Box on a Raft.
Was there no kinship in the bones that rest
Within these hulls to there or Mobile Bay?
The ships descended; men descended too.

Thomason is obsessed with blue ranks charging
The heights of Fredericksburg, the gray waves breaking
Upon the dykes at Franklin. Bataan fell;
After the flags were burned the death march started.
Around the curve of ocean a hundred isles
Entomb the battle dead from Mississippi,
From Texas prairies, plains of Illinois,
Virginians and New Yorkers side by side.

There was wild fighting in the woods at Shiloh,
Wilder among the rocks of Iwo Jima.
Simon Bolivar Buckner yielded Donelson;
Simon Bolivar Buckner died on Okinawa
By shell fire on the marge of victory.

Skip over to the far side of the world.
Uneasy waters rock four thousand ships,
Not Grecian ships along the coast of Troy,
And not the proud Armada that Drake harried,
Ships huge and tiny, graceful and grotesque,
Spewing from out their maws an iron seed,
Releasing men to breast a surf of flame,
Ships that make good the deed Napoleon planned,
The other way, taking an army over wave
Against a hostile shore to seize and hold.

Thomason thought of Stuart, Sheridan,
Thought not of Patton raging with his tanks
From Brittany through France. Here names are strange,
Cherbourg, St. Lo, Bastogne; far easier
Bull Run, Stone's River or the Wilderness.

Bemused with treasured conflict, Thomason dreamed
While nations fell, and tyrants waxed and waned,
Ignoring treacheries, onsets, deeds of arms,
High courage and the stubborn will to hold,
The dreadful pulse beat that may be the last
Great war that men will fight, not missiles.

Soon, soon a century will have passed
Since Beauregard let loose his fires on Sumter,
And then a hundred years since Appomattox!
These later battles lesser years ago
Also are history, distant, vague, unreal,
Like those once bleeding wounds, the Somme, Verdun,
Where Waterloo is one with Marathon.
What of their anguish, hate, endurance, grief?
Smoke of old camp fires, winds expiring breath.

Time sweeps away like the white wake of a ship
Into the darkness, bubbles on the foam,
And we forget, watch troubles of each day,
Dreading the shadow of a war to come.
Let the dead sleep in their world-scattered graves.
Courage is proven and fame may yet return
Though Thomason still writes of Gettysburg.

PRAYER

IN bed at night I wait on sleep,
And while my thoughts go wandering
I still a sort of vigil keep

To catch the moment sundering
The conscious thread, the snuffed out wick
That I await while wondering

Will I awake. Sleep is too quick;
I never note it when it's here;
I never somehow see the trick

Whereby it slips around my fear.
. . . .
From darkness, dreams obscure or queer,
May I still know the morning clear.

THE MAN WHO REALLY KNEW

THE man who really knew came to our town.
He had all answers if we only asked;
The why, the whence, and where could be unmasked;
This sunburned wanderer came from holy ground.
His clear, calm eyes probed all who stood around;
Truth, knowledge, power, like lights within them shone,
So friendly seeming yet so all alone!
His tales so daunting simple! Or profound?

Within the crowd a boy winked at a girl.
A cynic skeptic muttered: "Country hicks
Can swallow that." A woman felt a curl
And wondered did he notice, then broke in
To know if he could find her diamond pin,
While others sought his views on politics.

THE MAN WHO REALLY KNEW

II

His voice was noble, clear as a chiming bell;
(Bells can be tiresome when they chime too long)
His words were free as birds' flight, fluid, strong,
Precise to meaning, limpid as a well.
Were those who listened deaf, beneath a spell
That made them dumb and blind, thus dully wait
The sermon's ending, let its living spate
Pass like a cloud from which a few drops fell?

They did not know that what he spoke was law;
They could not see he opened wide a door
To worlds beyond; but I, I knew, I saw,
And yet I could not hold to what he said;
My thoughts went to and fro about my head
Like the blind ant I watched upon the floor.

REQUIEM FOR A CHURCH CONDEMNED

Lines written in the fall and winter of 1954-55
in the belief the building occupied by
the First Presbyterian Church would
shortly be sold and destroyed.

I

G EOMETRIC on the turquoise of the sky
The twin towers loom in brown solemnity.
As sunlight gilds their octagons and squares
Let us give thanks for buildings cleared away.
We see them now in these their latter days
As they were seen when all their bricks were new,
When they were greatest of the towers and spires
That stood above young Nashville. As the voice
Which preached within was dominant in town,
So they ruled all the sky line. Through the years,
Through summers hot as Egypt, through the smog
Of autumn morns, through equinoctial rains
That springtime brings, through the rare, drifting snow,
Subduing their hard angles into peace,
They stood and were the towers of the First,
The First Church, caring not for time and change,
The town grown city, clamor in the streets,
The grime descending.

                    A hundred years plus five
They watched their generations. Will they stand
Another hundred days? For they are doomed.
Their life is nearly death, as they await,
A simulacrum of what once was real,

74

Siege engines of the wreckers against walls
That no one guards and where no treasure is.

II

Recall their prime, recall the prompt design
To raise again the house of God that fire
Had gutted. It was modern then,
The plan that Strickland drew, so boldly plain,
Massively functional. But why Egyptian
Was questioned first as has been questioned since
Ten thousand times. A pagan temple? No.
The towers of Egypt still were towers for Christ.
The scholar elders knew their Bible well
Where Mizraim's name is next to Israel's,
The Egypt that knew Joseph, land that bred
The Israelites from families to tribes
For Moses, Prince of Egypt, to lead forth.
And ages later, when an humble man
Limped onward while the weary donkey bore
The Mother with the God Child in her arms
Where else but Egypt was their refuge found?

Why should Corinthian orders be more fit
(or Doric or Ionic, that once served
The petty brawling gods of Greece and Rome,
Fickle and fierce, unmoral as a cat)
To mark the worship of the Trinity
Than this austere design? For Presbyterians,
These building blocks stacked up beside the nave
Were firm as Calvin's logic, sure as faith,
Uncompromising as a Scottish hill,

So then as now, and in the years between,
The walls of Egypt still were walls for Christ.

III

These silent towers have known dark days before,
That morning when the pale faced messenger
Brought whispered word that Donelson had fallen,
And worship faltered, hurried to its end
Before the mob made riot in the streets;
The dragging months when beds replaced the pews
And wounded moaned and died where mingled well
Fever and filth, profanity and prayer.

Red letter days have these walls known also:
High moments; when the congregation first
Held worship in the basement, Easter Morn
Of dedication, the church turned back to God
With the war ended, the later pride-filled Morn
(Though some old members maybe stared aghast)
That hailed new decorations, side and rear
Resplendent in gay color, overhead
The squares of painted sky, to either side
The pulpit Aida backdrops drawn
Like Vendome scenery, Egypt's symbols used
All innocent of meaning—these replaced
The high simplicity that Strickland left,
Just as a walnut elegance replaced
With open curves, the old box pews with doors,
Taste of the eighteen-eighties, not our taste
Nor that of eighteen-fifty. We laugh now
At peacock tails in vases, the wax flowers

And bric-a-brac, yet that was a strong age.
Where we see doldrum calm, blew winds of change
Termed progress. Those bearded men were strong
Who sat upon the bench of elders then;
Deep was their faith in God and what he planned;
They looked ahead, not with the fear and doubt
That we now feel but in firm Christian hope;
Strict was their rule in judging right and wrong.

Yet maybe the best moments of this church
Were times no one recorded that each marked
A church's highest use: such glow lit hours
As solemn moments of a funeral
That said farewell and hail to a great soul;
A child's baptism, hallowed by the faith
Or parents and grandparents; moments when
The wedding march's deep diapason
Proclaimed one life, one love, again outpoured
The new wine blessing Cana's marriage feast;
And long remembered Sunday mornings when
The sermon was a sounding board for God
And light shone on the faces that filed out.
The impress of such moments haunts the walls
Like echoes of faint music never played,
A music dreamed of from eternity.

IV

Recall the voices muted, gone away,
That sounded from this pulpit, a long line
Of ministers, God's servants. Of them all
These marble tablets name the greatest three.
The first was he who laid the cornerstone,

The peer of Henry Clay as orator,
And yet no compromiser; all clear metal,
John Todd Edgar like a ringing bell
Called Nashville back to faith. Near thirty years
He walked these streets and built this church to greatness
And died, first citizen, saw nothing marred
Beyond the leaves of autumn, for death came
In the still hush before the guns of war.
Let Doctor Edgar be the voice of faith.

And second must be Thomas Verner Moore.
Was ever a brief pastorate so blessed?
Three years, the last a year of slowly dying,
Made him a legend, loving, Christlike, kind.
A church was named for him as well as children.
Let him be echo of the voice of love.

How shall I symbolize that third great man,
Whom I so well remember, James I. Vance,
That noble presence, awesome to a child,
Though softened by the kind eyes and the smile,
The arch type of the way the cloth should look?
Great preacher and good pastor, but to me
He chiefly typified the moral law,
The Ten Commandments moving in the flesh,
A prophet spirit crying out for God.

And with these three I now must rank a fourth
Of equal voice who also leaves his mark,
Walter Courtenay, Troubadour of God,
Making each prayer a poem, or a psalm.
In weaving his rich tapestries of words,
He throws the rainbow bridge of Christian hope

Beyond the grave. As beauty's servitor,
He ever seeks perfection not to be
Despite all change. On that first icy morn
His was the voice of unity and hope,
And now through strife and change how strange to seem,
Last of a mighty line, the voice of doom.

v

Doom and the end, why must they be? Because
Long years of change have slowly turned to gold
The earth beneath these stones until its worth
Has multiplied a thousand times the price
Randall McGavock took? Wealth must be used,
Not kept an idle talent? It may be,
Yet we must mourn who grew up in this house.

Should men love sticks and stones, old bricks and mortar?
Of course they must as tokens of what lies
Beyond, beneath the world we see and feel.
So long as we are prisoners of sense,
So long as we must touch things to believe,
A steadfast love needs tangibility.

The dream of what has been can tug as hard
As dreams of that to be. Both gild the lily;
Both add their overtones. The shining image
Of the new church spread out on Oak Hill lawns
Can only become real in bricks and mortar,
And being so made real, be made imperfect,
Be subject to the same mortality,
Change and decay, the leaks and stains of time,

The risk of passing fashion, obsolescence,
A neighborhood gone bad to mock its pride.
May it be just as sure of noble men
And women, the varied Christian lives,
To lend its beauty meaning, give it depth
As symbol of a great inheritance.

But how can this replace the gap we mourn
When Church Street will not know a single church
Except McKendree, last stronghold for God,
Serene behind its lawns? If it should go
The street should be renamed. Trade Street perhaps,
Or Fall Street. Never call it Spring again.

Churches should rise in green fields and the hills
Where children raise their children; churches bless
The blighted, sin cursed acres of the slums;
But should not churches also lift the cross
By the proud marble portals of finance,
Or where the merchants spread their glittering wares,
Where people work as well as where they live?
The church must be here first, a beachhead lost
Is costly to regain. This one is lost.

What ritual desanctifies a church,
Tears off the aura, makes space mundane, free
For cars to park, for bargains advertised,
Where once there were communion, hymn and prayer?
Will shoppers feel a strangeness as they pass
A bargain counter where the pulpit stood?

If God has willed an end, why has He not,
As twice before on this site, sent the flames

High leaping to proclaim His judgment day?
Two fires within two decades, none within
A century! Every violent force
Of storm, tornado and the chance of war
Have left these towers standing till our time,
Who vote their end. The congregation trades
The old for new, like trading in a car
Which must be junked, and of this what remains?
A brass plate and the memories of old men.
The church bell tolls the church's funeral.

VI

The bell tolls more than this; more will remain
Than we can see or touch. Our bitter questions
Apply to all things moving in the world.
The actors and the scenes wherein they move
Alike must fade out in an endless change.
The hills are not eternal and the sea
Will not keep always in its ancient bounds.
Where Nashville is was once a Shawnee town,
And long before, a dim forgotten race
Left crowded graves around deserted mounds.
Their bones and tools lie still beneath our feet,
Where Nashville was, who knows what once will be?

There was a temple stood on Zion's hill
Nebuchadnezzar took; one Ezra knew
Went down to clear the way for Herod's pride,
The gold and marble glory Jesus wept for,
Foreseeing the desolation Titus made.
Can lesser walls escape the bite of time?

As a tree falls by storm or by the axe,
Next month, next year or in a hundred years
This building here must topple in its hour.

When is "too soon"? Should buildings have a span
More fixed than men? The strong man in his prime
Dies suddenly with all his work half done,
And who knows why, or why a young girls dies,
As cancer chokes in bud the bloom and fruit?
The young at heart and faded wraiths of men
All sleep in graves alike, and near them lie
The tiny graves of sixty years ago
When children ran the gauntlet of disease
To fall so often. Yet on the little graves
Stand angels or a lamb, marks of the Church.

The question is not really why things end;
The question is are endings merely endings,
Or beginnings also? To this last
The Church proclaims a great affirmative,
Maintains, despite all doubt, with stubborn faith
There is an answer where no answer seems.
Wherever a church stands, antique or new,
Shabby or fine, no matter what the creed,
Its standing holds that endings are beginnings,
That paths are straight if we could only see,
And, if we cannot, its light cuts the fog
To guide us on through dimness to pure air.
Perhaps a lighthouse falls to make more clear
The Way, the Truth, the Light; a paradox,
But paradox is essence of our faith.
Cannot we then believe of buildings too
What once was here, what lived within this shell

Endures although the shell may break to bits?
Endings are one, beginnings myriad;
One flower dies to let a hundred seed
Be scattered, and some fall on fertile ground.

The Church is not the building! No it's not,
But neither is the present membership.
The Church must be a thing of fluid change
Living from past to future through each day.
The dead are still its members linked through us
To members yet to be, as in our frames
The cells renewing keep identity.
My image fails because the dead still live
Around us in the Church invisible
Which links us all in one continuum
Half light, half darkness; which is which depends
Upon the side we look from. They join us
In all our courts and meetings, know our plans.
These higher members, clouds of witnesses
Who watch us from the heavenly galleries
May grieve at our disputes and our despairs,
A loving happy grief. They cannot blame;
They only bless the ends our errors seek;
And they bless all alike, those who defend
Against great odds the holy place and work
Upon this corner that our fathers knew;
And those who think its sacrifice worth while
To build a greater work on Franklin Road,
Blessing alike the other churches sprung
From this one, and old members scattered far,
All still together in the great design
That shapes God's purpose and our destiny.

Standing or gone, moving or in this place,
The church that was, the church that will be IS,
A testament and witness to the Truth
That started with a dark ending on a hill,
The blackest ending of a shameful death
To pledge new hope beginning from a tomb.
For the great Church endures though buildings change.
Down dim, far vistas of the future years,
A timescape endless toward eternity,
Better or worse whatever they may be,
On garden cities of a tranquil world
Or iron strongholds of a new dark age
Still leans the shadow of a living Cross.

Stately and calm against a sapphire sky
The church towers dream in their brown revery.
Is it today, or thirty years ago?
The moment seems eternal. White wings gleam
As startled pigeons circling at the bell
Come drifting back to tread quadrilles of Spring.
Destruction waits; all hawks are far away.
The future may be changed, the past is safe;
All that was hallowed here is safe in time.
The solemn bell peals hope and peace and love.

WORDS

Words are a magic; words of beasts made men.
Words can make music, either bless or curse.
Words are the seeds that hold, as in a purse,
All time tried wealth of knowledge, so again
We living share the things the long dead ken.
In words no longer spoken, chanted verse
Built up an epic splendor to rehearse
The deeds of kings who held swords but no pen.

And yet words mock us. All we try to say
Seems naught, so tarnished, twisted, odd;
Our pledge to love or truth is but outcry
Of platitude or singsong. When we pray
We parrot unknown tongues, so only God
Translates our babble through his charity.

I WOULD GIVE THANKS

I OFFER thanks of course for major things:
For daily bread, my home's sequestered hours,
For those who share these, love that ever rings
My days, the spring upsurge of flowers;

For faith, for work, its recompense; and yet
I'm thankful too for things ephemeral;
Sky and a river red from a sunset,
Trudging with Ellen through a soft snowfall;

For casual scenes remembered from the past,
One dawn's proud sky, a window watch on rain;
No reason to remember, but they cast
Their pictures on my mind and there remain;

A scene at breakfast, Mother laughing, Dad
Intent upon his paper, First World War;
A lonely evening in the autumn, sad
Because a dog I loved had wandered far.

Give thanks for memories; men and women gone
Who were once good and kind and winsome in their ways,
Not tranced beneath the stones of a green lawn,
But living, moving, speaking from far days.

I'm thankful too for such a passing chance
As a young girl's smile that was not meant for me.
Her beauty come alive in one quick glance,
All youth eternal in one memory.

Thanks for great mercies, yes, but keep me saying
Thanks for the night song of a mockingbird.
Things random, gone, a glimpse of children playing
Through a train window, a moment viewed not heard.

And also I give thanks for books not read,
Places not seen, for friends I barely knew,
For work not done, for all the words unsaid,
Hopes unfulfilled in days that are too few.

ONCE

ONCE men looked out upon an unknown sea,
  Shadowed in mist and hurling waves headlong
Upon a western shore. Some, wise, or strong,
Would learn, beyond the waste, what there might be,
The edge of ocean falling thunderously,
Or monstrous shapes of death for time's eclipse;
Yet they would know, and so the little ships
Opened their wings to chance their destiny.

And after long months, mingled, storm and calm,
Some found, instead of death, a vast green land,
New continents and islands far withdrawn,
Fair and so fresh, the very air was balm,
Earth rich, tree tall, an Eden made for man
To explore, conquer, breed new nations on.

AND WILL BE?

Now men look out into the deeps of sky,
   Scanned from afar through all its maze of lights;
And some now dream to pierce its depths or heights,
In ventures far beyond where wings can fly;
Past moon and planets to the wastes that lie
Outside the sun's outriders; In a case
Of capsuled Earth, flame rocketed through space,
To ask again Man's endless "whence and why?"

The moon once reached, what joy will we attain?
Death walks the cinders of a burnt out shell
Where has been naught to die; the heavens rain
Only the Satan fall of meteors.
We would annex bleak emptiness of Hell,
And raise up demons for our heritors.

Now both the moons have gone; the air is cold,
    November crisps the leaf within the hedge.
Here, close to home, there still exists the wild,
A peace not desert, lonely but alive,
The calm of sleeping life, the mouse, the mole,
The pupae waiting spring beneath the grass,
Acre of night, compact of quietness.
Birds murmur in the hedges as I pass.
Step softly. Let them sleep, head under wing.
The dew is close to frost but steeps away,
A moment, fears and frets of worrying.
Those clouds will hide us, safe from any spying
Out of the rigid sky. Here in this shadowed place,
Think not of measured tickings out of space,
Better the voices of the kildees crying.

THE FLESH OF FLOWERS

THE flesh of flowers is firm, so cool and smooth.
Thick petals of the tulips mold their vases.
The plastic curvatures of daffodils
Are crisp and stiff before the winds of spring.
Even translucence of an iris petal
Maintains erect its threefold trinity.
So clean and firm, so cool and smooth, they feel
Like fluid marble—soft as children's skin,
No bone beneath but rippling ligament.

Colors are clear and crisp in cups of yellow,
Saucers of red, in globes and stars of blue,
Intricacies of shading bled between;
Florets piled up composite, goldsmith's work.
No man made flowers can truly copy these,
In substance firm, in sharp, detailed design,
Yet living, lifted up out of the earth,
A miracle unfolded, tangible.

Yet this firm stuff is also passing frail.
So sure and proud the flowers lift their heads
For such brief hours, a day, or so few days.
The time alloted runs out (who sets it),
And this integument, so crisp and strong,
Collapses, melts or withers, dies away;
Is paper like, or pulp between one's fingers.
The leaves doze on untroubled in the sun,
Under the rain, to vegetate through summer,
Building the strength to lift up flowers again
When winter leads the cycle back to spring.

Where ever they are called, the flowers stand
Like clansmen doomed by vows not to retreat.
Theirs is a courage passive, braving fate.
Crushed by a foot, or plucked and thrown away,
Nought shatters their deep innocence and calm.

Their weapons are the hidden roots and seed.
These are two powers that keep an endless life,
Endless at least till soil and climate change;
The power of roots that probe and spread beneath;
The power of seed that drift on winds above,
Or scatter round the stalks that gave them birth,
Hiding in cracks or borne away by streams
Born of the rain; but neither power could be
If flowers did not open up their faces
To greet the sun for their specific time.

One day or five, what matters? When they wither
The bumblebees sense other flowers beyond
And blunder on with pollen laden fur.
So beauty needs the beast to bring more flowers.
How firm their flesh before their passing day,
Fresh, yet so soft, like childhood's velvet skin,
The muscles smooth, unwearied in their youth.
How, as the wind goes by, the bright heads wave
Like children, joyous, dancing in the sun.

THROUGH THE WINDOW

For a bribery of fat and seed
    The birds come close to where I heed,
Their take-offs, landings from my window.
Outside a few chance flakes of snow
Drift idly by. The sky is gray,
The stones are gray, the grass gray-brown,
That box bush dark, but this back ground
Is quick with birds that flit and hop
In changing color for the sop
I spread for them upon the terrace.
Old customers who know the place
And shy newcomers seek their ration;
Window box and feeding station
All have their trade. Too often come
These immigrants I wish were home:
The frowsy sparrows, fighting, eating;
The dumpy pale-beaked starlings, beating
Their tarnished metal wings, that tear
At the lumps of suet hanging where
I planned for woodpeckers and wrens.

I grudge this waste until descends
The leaven of a cardinal,
A towhee, and the soft gray ball
The mockingbird can make himself
He soon becomes the jaunty elf
Of lifted wings and flaunting tail.
Who dances briefly, then sets sail
To steal red berries from my holly.
Others, in gray clothes too, are jolly

Despite the cold. The chickadees
Flit back and forth from box to trees
With sunflower seed to tap apart.
How could creation, chance or art,
Evolve them or that tiny jest,
Sir Titmouse with his feathered crest,
Another tree top harlequin.
Strange that crest should not mean kin,
Cardinal, titmouse, and that woodpecker,
Seen only once, the big bark wrecker,
The black and white, the pileated
With scarlet crest. These *are* related:
Red-bellied, sapsucker, downy, flicker;
Waiting their turn while starlings bicker.
Some birds to suet, some to seed
According to taste or avian need.

Beside the English sparrows I note
The white-streaked heads of the white throat,
With whisper songs of Canada,
And juncos who have come as far.
A jay is strident while his blue
Is vibrant with the redbird's hue;
Softer the grayed tones of the doves;
And then there are my special loves,
The towhees, black and chestnut brown,
The smart wife in her two-toned gown,
The towhees, well groomed, debonaire.
I watch, in hopes that something rare
May join these daily regulars.
Yonder a glint of yellow stirs

The shrubbery? Sit back. Nothing more
Than a myrtle warbler known before.

If I grow bored, the birds are too;
They drift away. Yonder a few
Are gleaning from the chilly sod
Some sustenance that comes from God,
Who counts the sparrows, not from me.
With nothing special now to see,
My mind goes wandering. Come May,
That warbler'll be near Hudson Bay,
And back will come his summer cousin,
Gold for my garden, now deep in
The forest caverns of Brazil.
Those jeweled atoms! Fierce the will
That spins the warblers twice a year
Over the salt leagues, makes them steer
From tropics to the arctic's edge
Where nestlings first knew tree or sedge.
The warbler's passage decks the Spring
With all their springtime patterning
Of blue and black and gold and gray.
But spring seems very far away.

As this thought fades, the sun comes out,
And birds take notice. All about
Come, tentative, the bits of singing,
Next, wrens with varied voices ringing,
While also sings a cardinal.
The bluebird drops his passing call,
Like bells that fall in water, then—
The chorus, swelling, wakes again

My dreams of spring and summer weather
And thoughts of birds that flock together,
Or wander solitary where
All life zones spread their deeps of air.
From beaches, tundras, forests, mountains,
Dim tangles by the bubbling fountains
The cool North hides, lands under sun,
From lotus swamps or deserts dun,
Thicket and park-land, tree tops airy
The unafraid, the ever wary.
The bird kind of each hemisphere
Of earth and ocean all appear
Within my whirling mind where dance
Tanagers and cormorants,
Condors and hummers, guillemots,
Parrots and crossbills, limpkins, knots.
New Guinea birds of paradise
And quetzals trapped for sacrifice
In Maya temples. I am dazed
With this phantasmagoria, mazed
With wings and tails and beaks and eyes,
The change of tint and hue that lies
Within the feathers' web and vane.

Back to my winter day again.
I shake the feathers from my head,
And note once more before me spread
My winter birds. The scene is one
Through past years often gazed upon.
These cardinals are not, I know,
Those fed here twenty years ago,
Yet keep the oneness of their breed.

Then there was seed and here is seed,
And up from death is life abundant.
I taste a richness, not redundant,
From samples seen, from samples heard
Out of infinity of bird.

BELLEEK VALENTINE

THE outside milk, the inside cream
Thin as the tissue of a dream,
The cunning work of Irish art,
This cream and sugar hold my heart.

Like you and I they form a pair,
Sitting on the table there;
Fragile as our human breath,
Firm as love that knows no death.

Each morning that you use them may
Some memories come of all the way
We've walked together, love of mine;
So take this china valentine.

TO A PORTRAIT OF ELLEN

IT's you, the you that I have loved so well,
And yet not quite, the jaw a shade too strong,
The lips too set. The mood? Not so much wrong
As rare. Wide eyes and mouth should smiling tell
Your joy in friends, in living. Here a spell
From that strange garden stops the come and go
Of busy errands, till days overflow,
That loyalty or conscience may impel.

The years will leave her changeless in this pose.
Know, you who won't remember, thus was she
In mirror loveliness, but more, much more
The inner beauty. How could art keep score
On young and old to whom her kindness goes,
Or draw her faith, her truth and modesty?

Notes

EARLY POEMS
1922–1926

Page 11, To a Tired Clerk. This is put at the beginning, not because it was written first, but because it summarizes in a way the sort of subject matter that moved me during the Fugitive period.

Page 13, Consider the Heavens. This was the first poem written after I became a Fugitive. My cousin, Ridley Wills, who had been taken in at the same time, chose the subject and challenged me to write a poem on it. He produced one which was facetious. Mine typically, turned out serious. After it appeared in *The Fugitive* I was rather surprised to get a complimentary letter about it from my pastor, Dr. Vance.

Page 15, Arlington National Cemetery. One of a group written for English 15.

Page 20, Fear. The two sonnets entitled Fear were concerned with the first mental illness of my Father, which was marked by a very profound but causeless depression. Someone who later saw them said they were rhetorical without developing any motivation, but to me this was the very point. There was no adequate explanation for a mental tragedy.

Page 22, Dream. In looking through a copy of *The Fugitive* for December, 1924, I discovered what I had forgotten—that I had rewritten or condensed this poem into a sonnet. I prefer the longer original version.

Page 27, Aunt Minnie. The person pictured in these three sonnets was not a real one. They represent a composite of two different persons with additions and exaggerations.

Page 30, Automobile Ride. This poem, with its rather monotonous beat, had a peculiar origin. One hot night I could not sleep because it pounded itself through my head, line by line, and over and over again. I was not consciously trying to create; rather I wanted to go to sleep but it would not let me. A few lines would come to me and then be repeated with additions. This would be joined on to a similar section, and the whole would be repeated over again from the beginning. Sometimes the process would bog down, but it would always manage to start again, and this continued until the Ride was finished. The next day I wrote it down, in large measure as it is now. At least this is the way I remember it, and also I remember being somewhat puzzled or disturbed by the way the poem came to me.

Page 35, BAT MAGIC. In this poem, and in PRIMAVERA, I used the word "mazda" as meaning a light bulb. At the time these mostly bore this trade name, adapted from the Persian god of light. The bulbs were of clear glass then so that the filament could be seen glowing inside. They rather fascinated me, though perhaps this was because of the name. I remember I wrote an early poem about "Strange fire eggs of crystal."

Page 40, A FUNDAMENTALIST. This poem and TRINITY, which follows it, were written at the time of the Scopes Trial, on the teaching of evolution, at Dayton, Tennessee.

Page 48, TO THE BUGLE UNBLOWN. I do not know the exact date of this, but it was written well after *The Fugitive* stopped publication and is perhaps the last serious poem I wrote for many years.

LATE POEMS
1953–1958

Page 51, REVERY. I put this first in this section because it was the first to be produced in my later period of writing. It started with two lines which popped into my head:

"A parrot preens upon a tropic isle,
Burning one flame of color no one sees."

and the rest was built more or less experimentally or artificially upon these. I have found that poems often start like this. Sometimes lines of verse will come to my mind when there is no opportunity to write them down, and usually they cannot be recalled later.

Page 54, QUESTION MARK AND ELEGY. This poem and the sonnet THE WATCHERS were written to accompany a long paper (or series of papers since it had various parts) on the American Indian and American Prehistory, which I read both at the Old Oak Club and the Coffee House Club in 1956. The long poem was inspired by a quotation from Sir Francis Palgrave, which I found in Thruston's *Antiquities of Tennessee:* "We must give up that speechless past, whether fact or chronology, doctrine or mythology, whether in Europe, Asia, Africa or America; at Thebes or Palenque, on Lycian Shore or Salisbury plain; lost is lost; gone is gone forever.

Page 60, SALUTE TO T. L. T. He was Thomas Leigh Thompson, who was my uncle by marriage. He and my aunt had no children of their own, and in my childhood and youth he was like a second father to me. He carried through a very long life a serenity and strength which I always admired.

Page 74, REQUIEM FOR A CHURCH CONDEMNED. I hesitated for a long time whether or not to include this. It is both topical and controversial since it relates to a recent division in the church to which I belonged. Also, events did not develop as I had expected. On the other hand, the poem is the longest and most ambitious I have written. It grew, rather than being deliberately planned, out of very profound and intense emotions which deeply stirred me. While the lines show a mixture of feelings, they were not intended to express either bitterness or animosity. In consideration of all this, and because I still find value in parts of the poem, I finally decided to print it. I might comment on one line which involves a sort of pun. Church Street in Nashville was originally called Spring Street because of a very large spring in the river bluffs at its foot.

ADDENDUM

This second printing permits me to add a few comments to the notes which I regretted omitting from the first printing.

The church referred to in *Requiem for a Church Condemned* was built in 1849 according to the designs of William Strickland, who was architect for the Tennessee State Capitol. It was in the Egyptian style which had a brief popularity at the time. In 1882 the auditorium was redesigned, with even more pronounced and rather flamboyant Egyptian decorations.

During the period of more than a century when the First Presbyterian Church used this building it was the outstanding Presbyterian church in Nashville, and practically all the other churches are offshoots from it. The building was not torn down. After the First Church congregation decided to move to the suburbs it agreed to sell the building to a minority within its ranks, which is now organized as the Downtown Presbyterian Church.

The poem *November, 1957,* on page 90, was written shortly after I had watched the first Russian Sputnik, or rather the rocket sleeve of the Sputnik, pass over my house one cold November evening. The two preceding sonnets, *Once* and *And Will Be?,* were also written at the same period, though a little later. At the time I had no idea that the exploration of space would develop so fast. I have never particularly wanted to be timely, but the times seem to catch up with me. I wrote the poem *The Survivors,* on page 44, somewhere around 1923. There was an intimation that two people were left after some vast and undescribed catastrophe. Very recently the thought in the last lines has been used over and over in jokes and cartoons.

THE POEMS in this book are set in 12-point
Fairfield type. Larger sizes of Deepdene are
used for the initial letters, for the title page,
and to head the sections. The book was
designed by Robert McGaw. It was
set, printed, and bound in Nashville by the Parthenon Press.